Contents

KB103006

Unit 1 · Who Do You See?

■ **Listen to the story.**　　　■ **Listen and circle.**

Look! Lots of friends are having fun!
Who do you see?

①

bat

I see a **b**at sleeping in a **b**ed.

②

pig

I see a **pig** eating in a pigpen.

③

duck

I see a **duck** swimming in a pond.

④

tub

I see a dog taking a bath in a **tub**.

⑤

ant

I see an **ant** shooting an **arrow**.

⑥

cat

I see a **cat** wearing a blue **cap**.

⑦

Wow, lots of friends are having fun indeed!

⑧

A Listen and repeat.

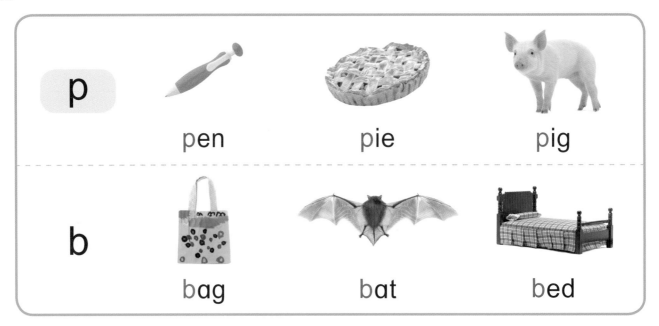

p	pen	pie	pig
b	bag	bat	bed

B Listen and circle the beginning letters.

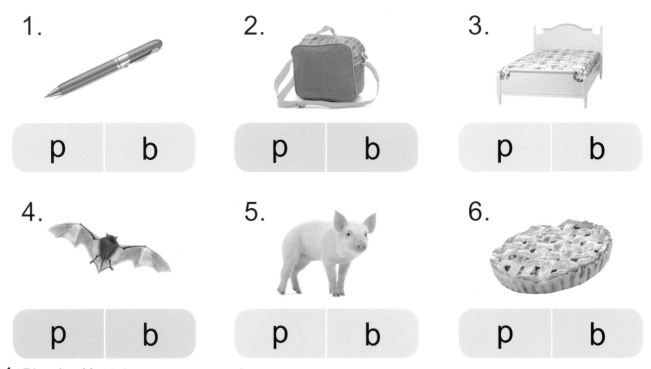

1. p   b

2. p   b

3. p   b

4. p   b

5. p   b

6. p   b

C Listen, write, and match.

1.   en • •  pen

2.  ed • • bat

3.  ig • • bed

4.  at • • 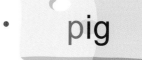 pig

D Listen and connect.

1.

b	en
p	ag

2.

b	ie
p	ad

3.

b	at
p	en

4.

b	ig
p	an

5.

b	on
p	en

6.

b	ed
p	ie

E Find and place the stickers.

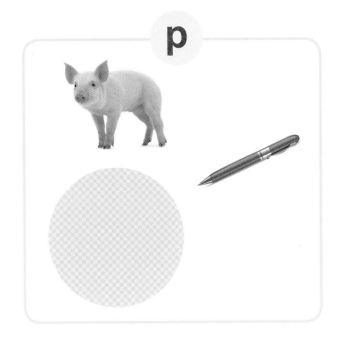

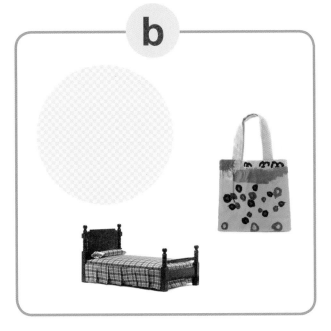

 F Find and place the stickers. stickers 2

1.    ___ p ___   +   **ig**   →   ___ pig ___

2.   ___ ___   +   **en**   →   ___ ___

3.    ___ ___   +   **ed**   →   ___ ___

 H **Look, circle, and write.**

1.

bat   pen   pie

I see a _____ sleeping in a bed.

2.

bed   bag   pig

I see a _____ eating in a pigpen.

T3

A Listen and repeat.

t	ten	top	tub
d	dad	doll	duck

B Listen and circle the same beginning sounds.

1. tub

2. doll

3. ten

C Listen, circle, and draw.

1. tub   ten   top   doll

2. top   duck   tub   dad

D Listen and solve the maze.

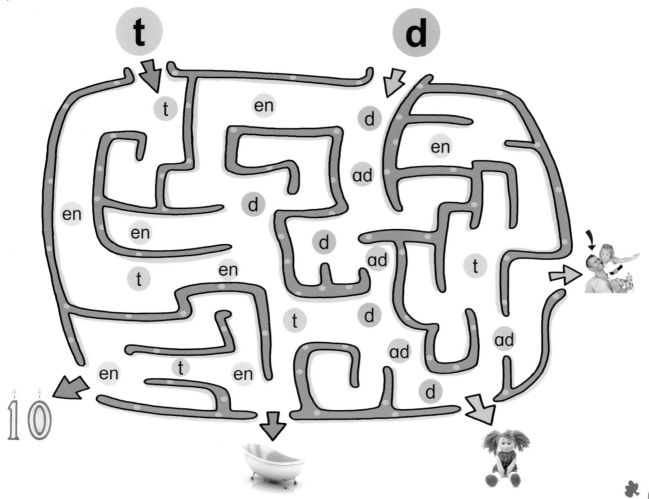

E Find and place the stickers. stickers 3

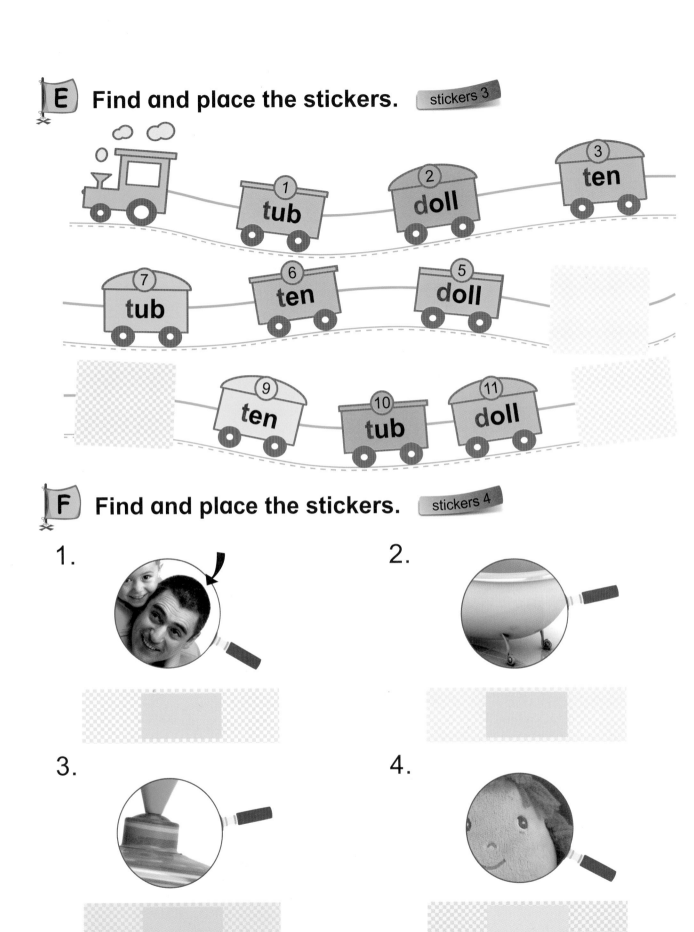

F Find and place the stickers. stickers 4

1.

2.

3.

4.

G Look, match, and trace.

1.

2.

3.

4.

t

d

ten   doll   top   duck

H Look, circle, and write.

1.

duck   ten   top

I see a _____ swimming in a pond.

2.

dad   tub   doll

I see a dog taking a bath in a _____ .

A Listen and repeat.

B Listen and number.

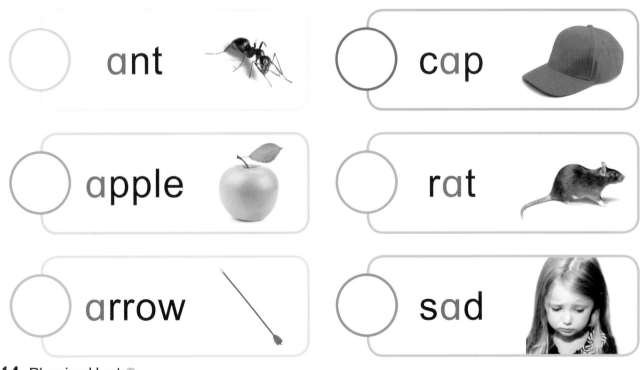

C Listen and write.

1.

a p p l e

2.
s _ d

3.
_ rrow

4.
r _ t

5.
_ nt

6.
c _ p

D Listen and circle.

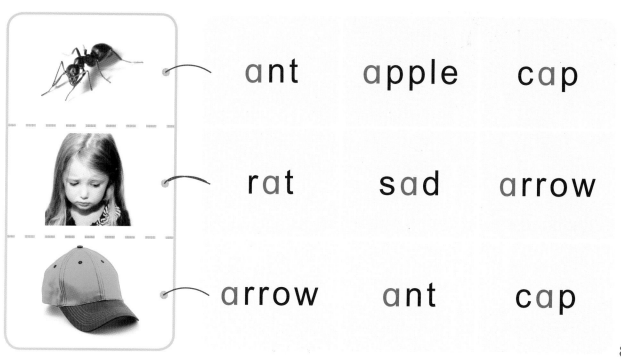

ant   apple   cap

rat   sad   arrow

arrow   ant   cap

E Find and place the stickers.

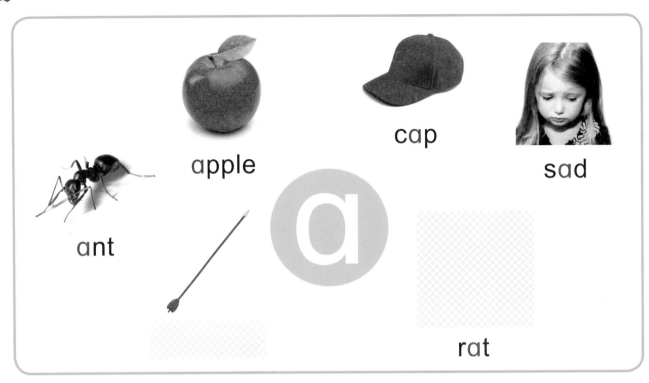

apple

cap

sad

ant

a

rat

 F Find and place the stickers.

G Look and write.

1.

a + ___ → ant

___ + nt → ___

2.

___ + a + ___ → cap

c + ___ + p → ___

3.

___ + a + ___ → rat

r + ___ + t → ___

H Look, circle, and write.

1.

sad   arrow   rat

I see an ant shooting an _____ .

2.

apple   cap   ant

I see a cat wearing a blue _____ .

Who Has a Fin?

■ **Listen to the story.**　　　■ **Listen and circle.**

 T5

Who has a **fin**?

fin

A **fish** has a **fin**.

1

Who has a **v**est?

vest

A **v**et has a **v**est.

2

Who wants **soup**?

soup

A **zebra** wants **soup**.

3

Who wants an **egg**?

egg

An **elephant** wants an **egg**.

4

Who flies in a **jet**?

jet

My **pet** rabbit flies in a **jet**.

5

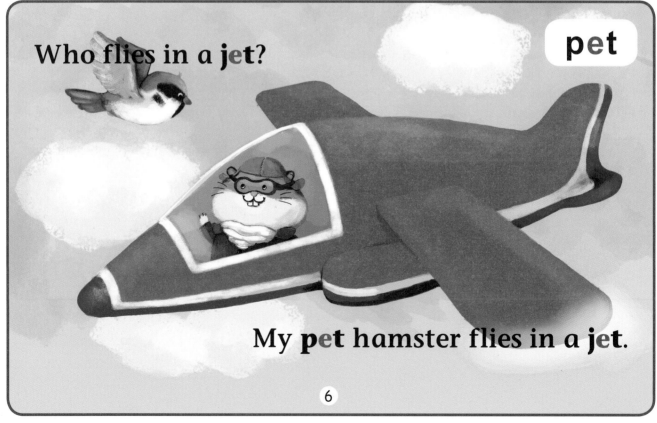

Who flies in a **jet**?

pet

My **pet** hamster flies in a **jet**.

6

Who has a **f**an?

fan

A fox has a **f**an.

⑦

Who has a **v**an? ♪

van

A monkey has a **v**an.

8

A **Listen and repeat.**

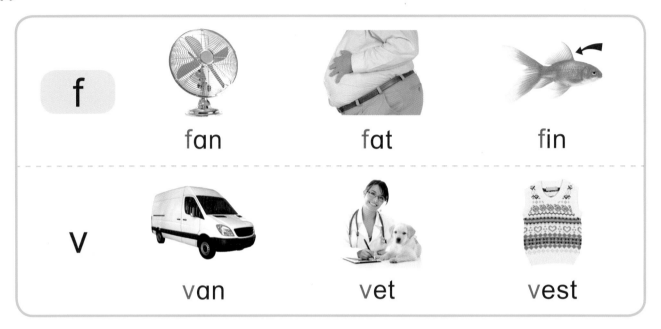

f	fan	fat	fin
v	van	vet	vest

B **Listen, number, and match.**

◯ van ◯ fin ◯ fan ◯ vest

C Listen and circle.

1.   fin   fan   fat

2.   van   vest   vet

D Listen, write, and match.

1.

at •   • vet

2.

est •   • vest

3.

et •   • fin

4.

in •   • fat

E **Find and place the stickers.** stickers 1

v	f
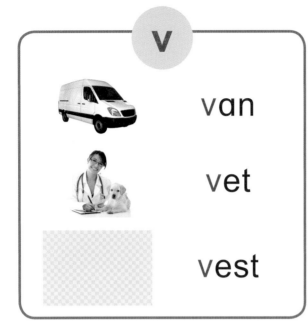 van	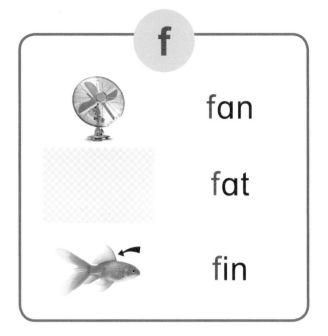 fan
vet	fat
vest	fin

F **Find and place the stickers.** stickers 2

G Look, match, and trace.

1.    2.   3.    4.

f   v

vet   fin   vest   fat

H Look, circle, and write.

1.

van   fin   fat

A fish has a _____ .

2.

fan   vest   fat

A vet has a _____ .

② Consonants S & Z

A Listen and repeat.

S	sand	six	soup
Z	zebra	zero	zigzag

B Listen and circle the same beginning sounds.

1. zero

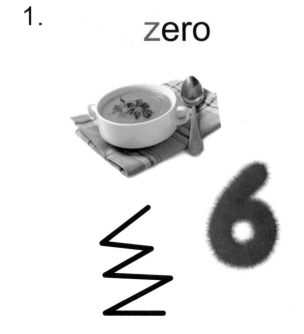

2. six

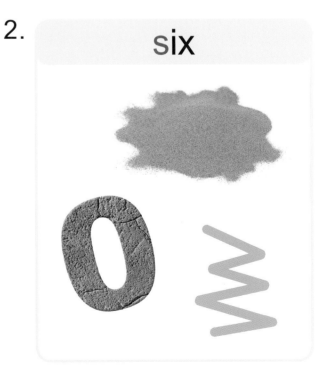

C Listen, circle, and trace.

1.

sand   six

2.

zero   zebra

3.

zigzag   zebra

4.

sand   soup

D Listen and solve the maze.

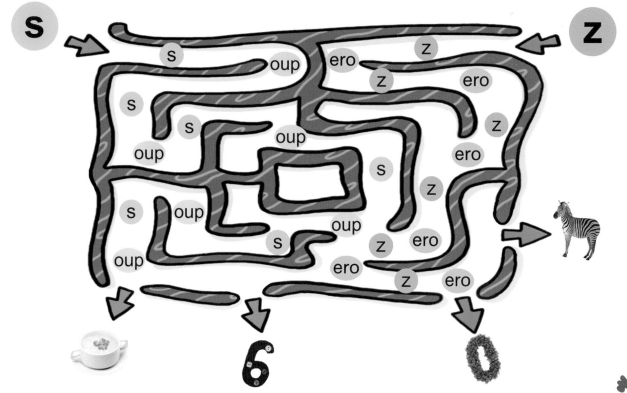

E Find and place the stickers. stickers 3

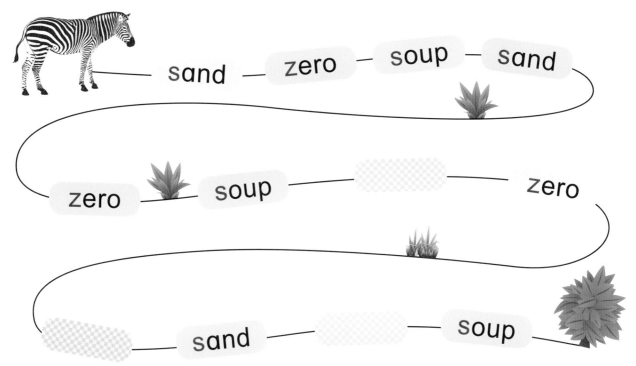

F Find and place the stickers. stickers 4

1.

2.

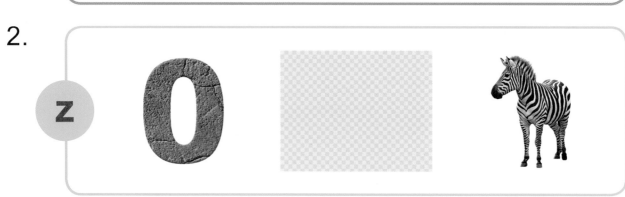

G Look and write.

1.   s + **ix** → six

2.   ___ + **ebra** → ___

3.  ___ + **oup** → ___

4.   ___ + **ero** → ___

H Look, circle, and write.

zebra   sand   soup   zero

A _____ wants _____ .

3 Short Vowel e

A Listen and repeat.

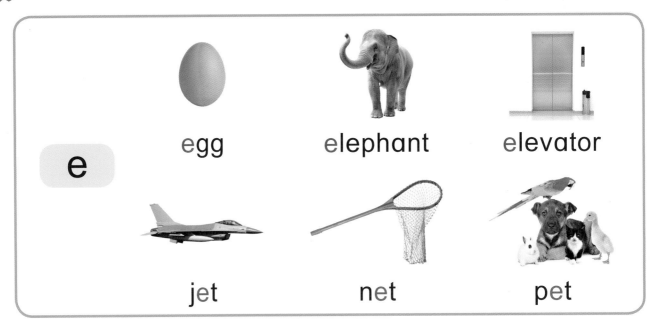

e

egg

elephant

elevator

jet

net

pet

B Listen and number.

egg

jet

elephant

net

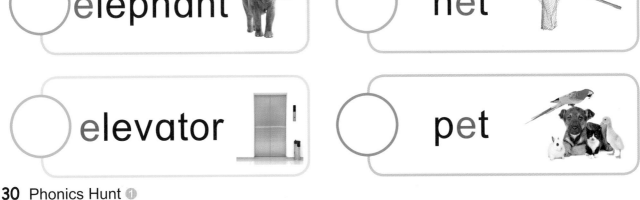

elevator

pet

C Listen, find, and circle.

1.  g n e t i k j b g n e t y z j k m n e t a q

2.  y r t w j e t b m s j e t z l p k j e t t g j

3.  b n z v x f h j e g g l m a q k i o e g g e

D Listen and connect.

1.

e	pple
a	lephant

2.

d	e	d
p	a	t

3.

j	a	t
s	e	d

4.

a	levator
e	rrow

E **Find and place the stickers.** stickers 5

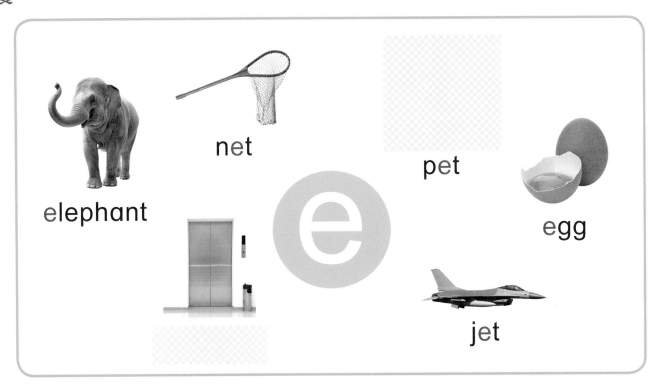

elephant

net

pet

egg

jet

 F **Find and place the stickers.** stickers 6

G Look and write.

1.

e + _____ → e g g

_____ + gg → _____

2.

_____ + e + _____ → p e t

p + _____ + t → _____

3.

j + _____ + t → j e t

_____ + e + _____ → _____

H Look, circle, and write.

jet　　elevator　　egg　　net

My pet rabbit flies in a _____ .

A Cleaning Day

■ **Listen to the story.**   ■ **Listen and circle.**   T9

Mom is busy cleaning the house.

①

Mom is using a **mop** to clean the floor.

②

mop

Shhhhh! The baby is taking a nap.

nap

3

There is a soft pink blanket covering his legs.

4

There is a big red juice stain on the **r**ug.

rug

⑤

There is a big black **i**nk stain on the sofa.

ink

⑥

There is a big white **milk** stain on the chair.

milk

⑦

She needs to clean them all up.
Mom is busy cleaning the house.

⑧

1 Consonants m & n

A Listen and repeat.

| m | map | mat | mop |
| n | nap | nest | nut |

B Listen and circle the beginning letters.

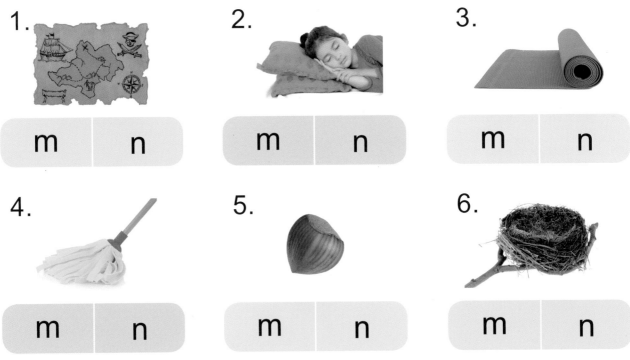

1.

m n

2.

m n

3.

m n

4.

m n

5.

m n

6.

m n

C Listen, write, and match.

1.    ut   mat

2.   at   nut

3.    ap   mop

4. 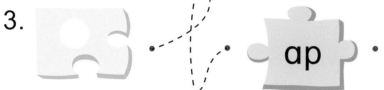   op   nap

D Listen and connect.

1.
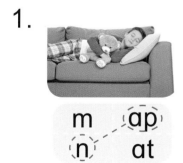

m   ap
n   at

2.
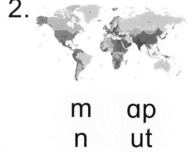

m   ap
n   ut

3.

m   est
n   op

4.
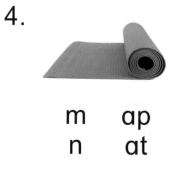

m   ap
n   at

5.
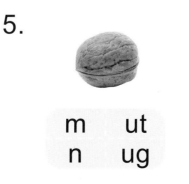

m   ut
n   ug

6.

m   op
n   ut

E Find and place the stickers.

 **m**

n

 F Find and place the stickers.

G Look and write.

1.  __m__ + **ap** → __m a p__

2.  _____ + **ut** → _____

3. _____ + **at** → _____

H Look, circle, and write.

1.

| nut | mop | nest |

Mom is using a _____ to clean the floor.

2.

| map | mat | nap |

Shhhhh! The baby is taking a _____ .

A Listen and repeat.

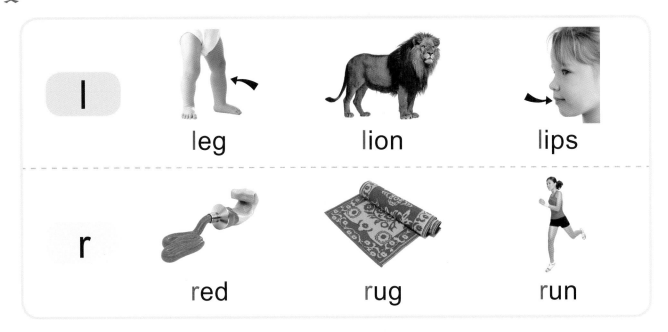

l leg lion lips

r red rug run

B Listen and circle the same beginning sounds.

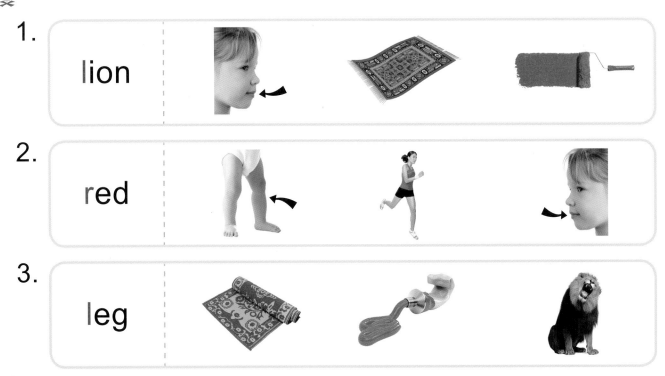

1. lion

2. red

3. leg

C Listen, circle, and draw.

1. lion   red   lips   run

2. leg   rug   lion   red

D Listen and solve the maze.

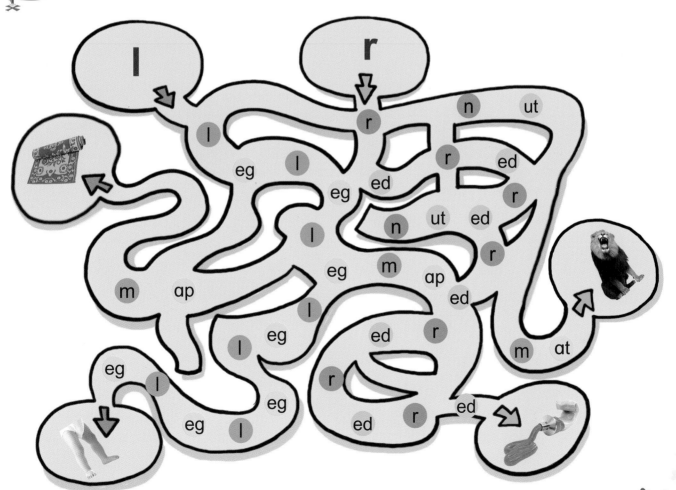

E **Find and place the stickers.** stickers 3

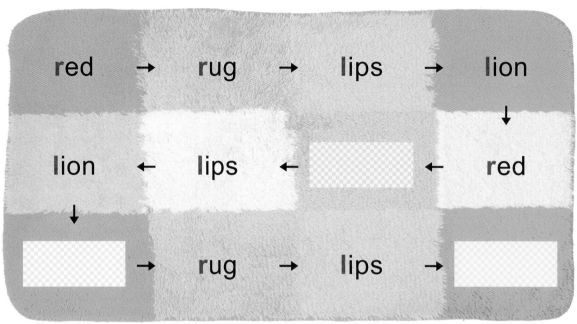

red → rug → lips → lion

↓

lion ← lips ← ____ ← red

↓

____ → rug → lips → ____

 F **Find and place the stickers.** stickers 4

1.

2.

3.

4.

G Look, match, and trace.

1.  2.  3.  4.

l

r

red   lion   run   leg

H Look, circle, and write.

1.

leg   run   red

There is a soft pink blanket covering his _____s.

2.

lion   rug   lips

There is a big red juice stain on the _____.

③ Short Vowel i

A Listen and repeat.

igloo	iguana	ink
hill	milk	wig

B Listen and number.

igloo

hill

iguana

milk

ink

wig

C Listen and write.

1.

w i g

2.

_ n k

3.

_ g u a n a

4.

m _ l k

5.

g _ l o o

6.

h _ l l

D Listen and circle.

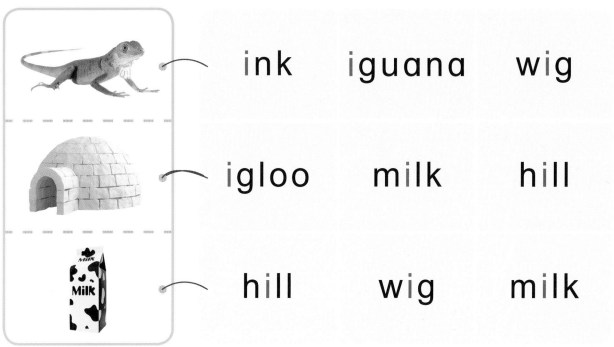

ink   iguana   wig

igloo   milk   hill

hill   wig   milk

E **Find and place the stickers.** stickers 5

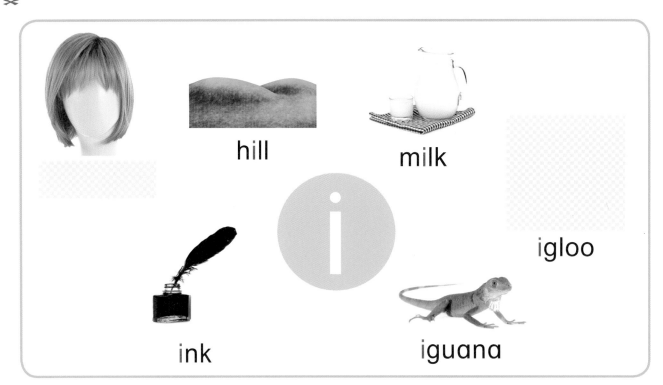

hill

milk

igloo

ink

iguana

 F **Find and place the stickers.** stickers 6

G Look and write.

1.

| i | + | | → | ink |
| | + | nk | → | |

2.

| | + | i | + | | → | wig |
| w | + | | + | g | → | |

3.

| | + | i | + | | → | hill |
| h | + | | + | ll | → | |

H Look, circle, and write.

1.

wig   ink   iguana

There is a big black _____ stain on the sofa.

2.

milk   hill   igloo

There is a big white _____ stain on the chair.

It's Time to Eat!

■ **Listen to the story.**   ■ **Listen and circle.**
T13

A king and a queen are having their meals.

1

The **king** is drinking orange juice.

king

2

The **q**ueen is drinking milk.

3

queen

The king is eating **h**am and eggs.

4

ham

The queen is eating toast with **jam**.

jam

The king likes **olives** in his salad.

olive

The queen likes hot soup in a **p**o**t**.

pot

7

The king and queen always enjoy their meals.

8

1 Consonants **k** & **q**

A Listen and repeat.

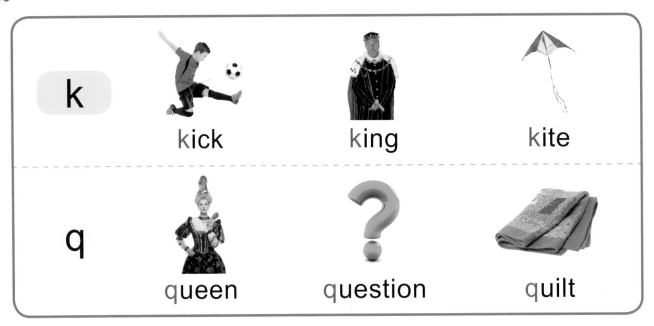

| k | kick | king | kite |
| q | queen | question | quilt |

B Listen, number, and match.

◯ kite ◯ question ◯ quilt ◯ kick

C Listen, circle, and draw.

1. kick   king   kite

2. queen   question   quilt

D Listen, write, and match.

1.   ick   · · king

2.   ueen   · · quilt

3.   ing   · · kick

4.   uilt   · · queen

E Find and place the stickers. stickers 1

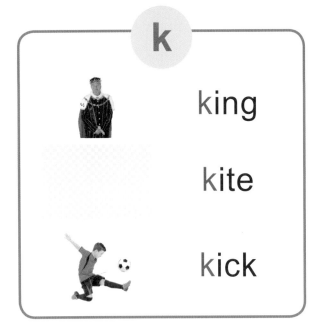

k	
king	
kite	
kick	

q	
queen	
question	
quilt	

F Find and place the stickers. stickers 2

G Look, match, and trace.

1. 　2. 　3. 　4.

k　　　　**q**

quilt　kite　question　kick

H Look, circle, and write.

1.

kick　king　kite

The _____ is drinking orange juice.

2.

queen　question　quilt

The _____ is drinking milk.

② Consonants **h** & **j**

Ⓐ **Listen and repeat.**

h	ham	hen	hot
j	jam	jar	jump

Ⓑ **Listen and circle the same beginning sounds.**

1. **hot**

2. **jar**

C Listen, circle, and trace.

1.

hen   jam

2.

hot   jump

3.

jump   jam

4.

hen   hot

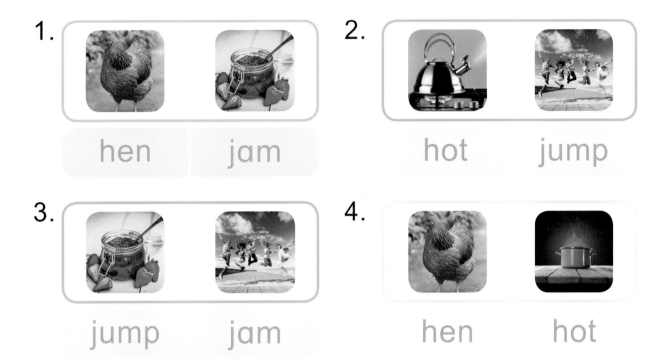

D Listen and solve the maze.

h   j

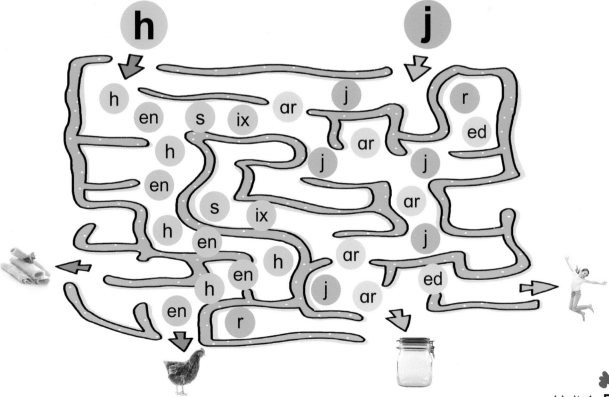

h
en   s   ix   ar   j   r
h   ed
en   ar   j
s   ix   ar   j
h   en   ar
h   en   h
en   h   j   ar   ed
r

E Find and place the stickers. stickers 3

hen — jam — hot — hen

hot — — jam

hot — hen — jam —

F Find and place the stickers. stickers 4

G Look and write.

1.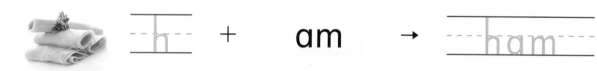
   h + **am** → ham

2.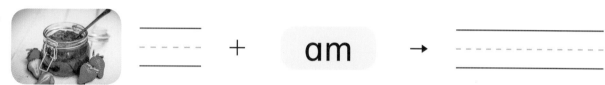
   ___ + **am** → ___

3.
   ___ + **ump** → ___

4.
   ___ + **ot** → ___

H Look, circle, and write.

1.

   ham   hen   jar

   The king is eating _____ and eggs.

2.

   jump   hot   jam

   The queen is eating toast with _____ .

3 Short Vowel o

A Listen and repeat.

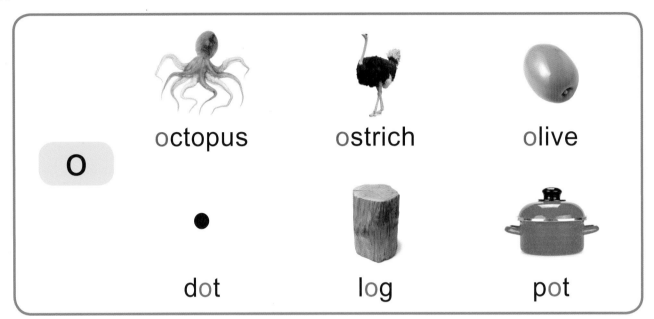

o

octopus   ostrich   olive

dot   log   pot

B Listen and number.

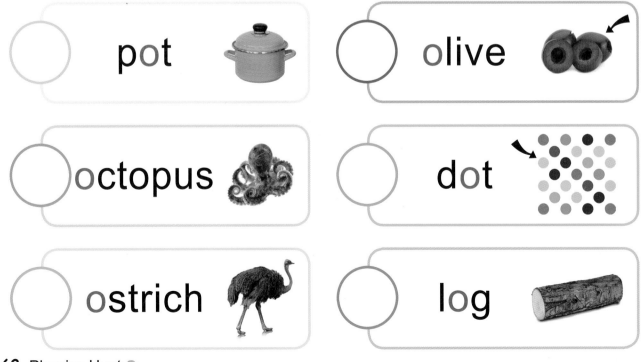

○ pot

○ olive

○ octopus

○ dot

○ ostrich

○ log

C Listen, find, and circle.

1.  g o l i v e x t d p k o l i v e g w o l i v e x

2.  t d s p o t s d l k j w p o t s z l q p o t p

3.  q w e x o t c d o t e c i v m l p d o t g l

D Listen and connect.

1.

l	e	g
t	o	n

2.

e	strich
o	lephant

3.

o	gg
e	ctopus

4.

f	o	n
p	a	t

E **Find and place the stickers.** stickers 5

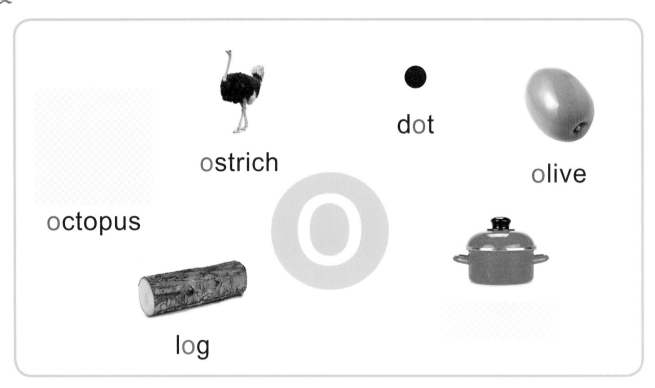

ostrich

dot

olive

octopus

O

log

 F **Find and place the stickers.** stickers 6

1

2

3

4

G **Trace and write.**

1.

o + → o l i v e

+ live →

2.

+ o + → d o t

d + + t →

3.

p + + t → p o t

+ o + →

H **Look, circle, and write.**

dot   octopus   log   olive

_____

The king likes _____s in his salad.

Phonics Song

⭐ **Sing a song.**

P is for   p p pen

B is for 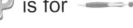   b b bat

T is for 10   t t ten

D is for    d d dad

F is for    f f fan

V is for   v v van

S is for **6**   s s six

Z is for **0**   z z zero

M is for 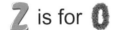   m m map

N is for    n n nut

L is for   l l leg

R is for    r r red

K is for    k k king

Q is for    q q quilt

H is for    h h hen

J is for   j j jam

Unit 1 Who Do You See?

p. 2~5

bat  pig duck

tub  ant cat

p. 6

B 1. p 2. b 3. b 4. b 5. p 6. p

p. 7

C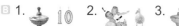

D 1. b-ag 2. p-ie 3. b-at
4. p-ig 5. p-en 6. b-ed

p. 8

E p.   b.

F 1. pig 2. bat

p. 9

G 1. p, pig 2. p, pen 3. b, bed

H 1. bat 2. pig

p. 10

B 1.   2.   3.

p. 11

C 1. tub ten (top) doll

2. top (duck) tub dad

D

p. 12

E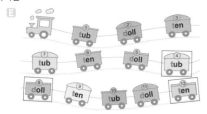

F 1. dad 2. tub 3. top 4. doll

p. 13

G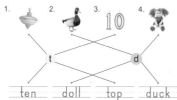

ten doll top duck

H 1. duck 2. tub

p. 14

B 5 → 3 → 2 → 6 → 4 → 1

p. 15

C 1. apple 2. sad 3. arrow
4. rat 5. ant 6. cap

D
(ant) apple (cap)
rat (sad) arrow
arrow (ant) (cap)

p. 16

E

apple   cap   sad

ant

arrow   rat

F 1. apple 2. ant

p. 17

G 1. a+nt → ant 2. c+a+p → cap
3. r+a+t → rat

H 1. arrow 2. cap

Unit 2 Who Has a Fin?

p. 18~21

fin   vest   soup

egg   jet   pet

fan   van

p. 22

B (2) van (4) fin (1) fan (3) vest

p. 23

C 1. fan   2. vet

D
1. v — at   vet
2. f — est   vest
3. v — et   fin
4. f — in   fat

p. 24

E v.   f.

F 1. fan 2. van

p. 25

G

vet fin vest fat

H 1. fin 2. vest

p. 26

B 1.   2.

p. 27

C 1. 6 2. 0 3.   4.
six zero zigzag sand

D  s   z

6   0

p. 28

E
sand — zero — soup — sand
zero — soup — sand — zero
soup — sand — zero — soup

F 1. 6 2.

p. 29

G 1. s, six   2. z, zebra
3. s, soup   4. z, zero

H zebra, soup

p. 30

B 6 → 2 → 1 → 5 → 3 → 4

p. 31

C 1. gne(net)ikjbg(net)yzjkm(net)aq

2. yrtw(jet)bms(jet)zlpk(jet)tgi

3. bnzvxfhj(egg)maqkio(egg)e

D 1. e-lephant 2. p-e-t
3. j-e-t   4. e-levator

p. 32

E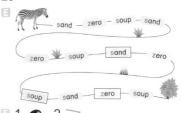
net   pet
elephant   e   egg
elevator   jet

F 1. egg 2. elephant

p. 33

G 1. e+gg → egg 2. p+e+t → pet
3. j+e+t → jet

H jet

Unit 3 A Cleaning Day

p. 34~37

mop  nap rug

ink milk

p. 38

B 1. m 2. n 3. m 4. m 5. n 6. n

p. 39

C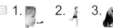

D 1. n-ap 2. m-ap 3. n-est
   4. m-at 5. n-ut 6. m-op

p. 40

E m. n.

F 1. nap 2. mop

p. 41

G 1. m, map 2. n, nut 3. m, mat

H 1. mop 2. nap

p. 42

B 1. 2. 3.

p. 43

C 1. (lion) red lips run

   2. leg (rug) lion red

D

p. 44

E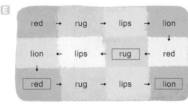

red	→	rug	→	lips	→	lion
lion	←	lips	←	rug	←	red
red	→	rug	→	lips	→	lion

F 1. lips 2. rug 3. lion 4. run

p. 45

G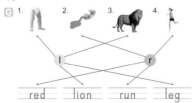
red lion run leg

H 1. leg 2. rug

p. 46

B 4 → 5 → 6 → 1 → 2 → 3

p. 47

C 1. wig 2. ink 3. iguana
   4. milk 5. igloo 6. hill

D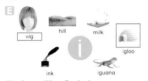
ink (iguana) wig
(igloo) (milk) hill
hill wig (milk)

p. 48

E
wig hill milk igloo
ink iguana

F 1. milk 2. ink

p. 49

G 1. i+nk → ink 2. w+i+g → wig
   3. h+i+ll → hill

H 1. ink 2. milk

Unit 4 It's Time to Eat!

p. 50~53

king queen ham

jam olive pot

p. 54

B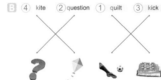
④ kite ② question ① quilt ③ kick

p. 55

C 1. kick king (kite)

   2. queen (question) quilt

D
1. q — ick — king
2. q — ueen — quilt
3. k — ing — kick
4. k — uilt — queen

p. 56

E k. q.

F 1. king 2. queen

p. 57

G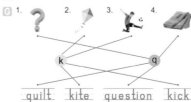
quilt kite question kick

H 1. king 2. queen

p. 58

B 1. 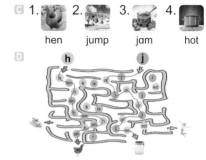 2.

p. 59

C 1. 2. 3. 4.
hen jump jam hot

D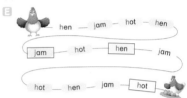
h   j

p. 60

E
hen — jam — hot — hen
jam hot hen jam
hot — hen — jam — hot

F 1. ham 2. jam

p. 61

G 1. h, ham 2. j, jam
   3. j, jump 4. h, hot

H 1. ham 2. jam

p. 62

B 5 → 2 → 6 → 1 → 3 → 4

p. 63

C 1. g(olive)xtdpk(olive)gw(olive)x

   2. tds(pot)sdlkjw(pot)szlq(pot)p

   3. qwexot(dot)ecivmlp(dot)gl

D 1. l-o-g 2. o-strich
   3. o-ctopus 4. p-o-t

p. 64

E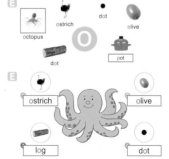
ostrich dot olive
octopus o
dot pot

E
ostrich olive
log dot

p. 65

G 1. o+live → olive
   2. d+o+t → dot
   3. p+o+t → pot

H olive